# Crossing the Divide

*Poems by*

# Megeen R. Mulholland

*Finishing Line Press*
Georgetown, Kentucky

# Crossing the Divide

Copyright © 2021 by Megeen R. Mulholland
ISBN 978-1-64662-682-3 First Edition
All rights reserved under International and Pan-American Copyright Conventions. No part of this book may be reproduced in any manner whatsoever without written permission from the publisher, except in the case of brief quotations embodied in critical articles and reviews.

## ACKNOWLEDGMENTS

Grateful acknowledgment is made to *Adanna Literary Journal* in which "Crossing the Divide" and "Foreshadowing" first appeared.


Publisher: Leah Huete de Maines
Editor: Christen Kincaid
Cover Art: "Scheduled Passenger Train Hurries Past," John J. Mulholland, Author's Personal Collection
Interior Photos: Author's Personal Collection
Author Photo: Rauri J. Mulholland, Author's Personal Collection
Cover Design: Elizabeth Maines McCleavy


Order online: www.finishinglinepress.com
also available on amazon.com

Author inquiries and mail orders:
Finishing Line Press
PO Box 1626
Georgetown, Kentucky 40324
USA

# Table of Contents

Survivors ................................................................. 1

Passage ................................................................... 4

Foreshadowing ...................................................... 6

lay the tracks, Jack! ............................................... 7

Family Tree ............................................................ 8

Crossing the Divide ............................................... 9

Proof ..................................................................... 11

"The Belle of Edenwald" ..................................... 13

Heart Failure ....................................................... 15

Hey, Dad .............................................................. 16

Top this! ............................................................... 18

Obituary ............................................................... 20

Plow ..................................................................... 22

Faithful ................................................................ 24

Wind Chill ........................................................... 26

Encircled by the Engraved Band ........................ 27

Landscaping ........................................................ 29

*For Dad*

**Survivors**

I sort out family slides
holding his images
up to the light as one
train car after another proceeds,
suspended in time, toward me—
engines, boxcars, and caboose
coupled and loose, riding miles
in his endless tracking of
divided and abandoned railway.

He documents how cars,
once separated from their engines,
are nudged over the hump
onto forked tracks,
coaxed over broken ties,
or rolled deliberately
into roundhouses for repair,
and turned out again
in the opposite direction
from where they had come.

He documents how still images of impact—
splintered wood against
iron dark as blood—
billow black steam,
coughing up the coal,
and beyond the point of contact,
how remaining cars are laid wide open
at odd angles to each other
since the head cab has
jumped the tracks.

Amid the chaos of the cars
are my brothers and sisters
smiling out of the etched
darkness of the Kodachrome
from the lattice safety of
playpens, padded cribs,

and ornate carriages—
they share frame after frame
with my mother and him,
all inextricably linked
at the elbows on trips,
leading, succeeding,
and waving from gates
in places I don't
recognize, and have
never been.

Within some compartments
of the narrow slide trays
are empty windows—
irregular sequences of light pass
over the screen, mesmerizing,
as if one erratic locomotive
races adjacent to a passenger car
endlessly delayed in the station.

Jarred from reflection
by the shrill whistle
of the expended projector,
I retract, and hasten toward
the end of the stack, trying to
load slides and trays in order,
but images of coach and child
become too familiar to distinguish,
even by year, which was taken
or born prior to the other.

Then, with the sudden
ease of family stories,
half-dismantled trays,
left momentarily, roll
back through the tipple

and off of the projector rails,
colliding with those already
lost in my outstretched arms
or overturned in my lap,
and I watch these descending
stills reverting to life—
the trains and children,
with their relentless momentum
of weight and emotion
bearing down and burying
the individual progression
I'd searched for, each
negative falling and
quickly eclipsing the next,
connecting in declining sequence,
parent, child, engine, boxcar, and crib
at such a clip that I give up,
allowing all to settle,
in exhaustion, at my feet,
as I rise above it,
only to descend again,
to sift for survivors,
hoping to find
a semblance of
myself among them.

**Passage**

When my mother sold
our childhood home
my brothers almost
came to blows
over what to keep
and what to give away.

My great aunt's steamer trunk
was among the possessions
over which they obsessed—
one saying it was
a piece of history
and must be preserved
since our family's heritage
had been carried within it—
the other saying it was
too far gone to salvage
and would only be a burden
to carry farther.

While they struggled
with it between them
I imagined the baggage handlers
on that immigrant ship
grip the thick leather handles
and heave it forward
onto the Irish heap
of steerage baggage
weighing down the lower deck—
my great aunts
wringing their hands,
sinking into the throng
as their linens and sentimental lace
were wrenched from them—

so much of the baggage
worn out through the passage
as their old things faded
in light of their new country
of endless opportunity
and earnest hope
in learning.

My elder brother
eventually won—
vowing to restore
the steamer as an heirloom
for future generations.

In the end,
he left it in the original
scripted paper lining
and veined leather casing,
the brass tacks
and heavy round latch
laden with his books
from the university on
archeology,
genealogy,
and philosophy.

**Foreshadowing**

He must have seen
his darkened figure
in the foreground
of the photograph
looming large before him
as he looked through the viewfinder,
standing off to one side of the track.

The abandoned passenger car
is filled with darkened figures
and bystanders who peer
through its windows from the outside
as if at an exhibit; they
climb aboard and disembark,
some shrugging away from the train
with indifference to history.

I wish I could step
from this long life's
seclusion and alight
with them, then surprise him
by turning toward the sun,
crossing the tracks, and
stepping into his shadow—
readjusting his focus

from this background
of black and white to
the tinge of color
foreshadowing our future.

**lay the tracks, Jack!**

lay the tracks, Jack!
clickety clack,
forward and back
you've got to stack
wood ties and steel
here, where you can feel
the earth beneath heave
with the weight of the rails
pound them down, Son,
joined end to end
I watch you pretend
you are the foreman
WHOOO! WHOOO! WHOOO!
sounding out a warning
from the back of the garden

# Family Tree

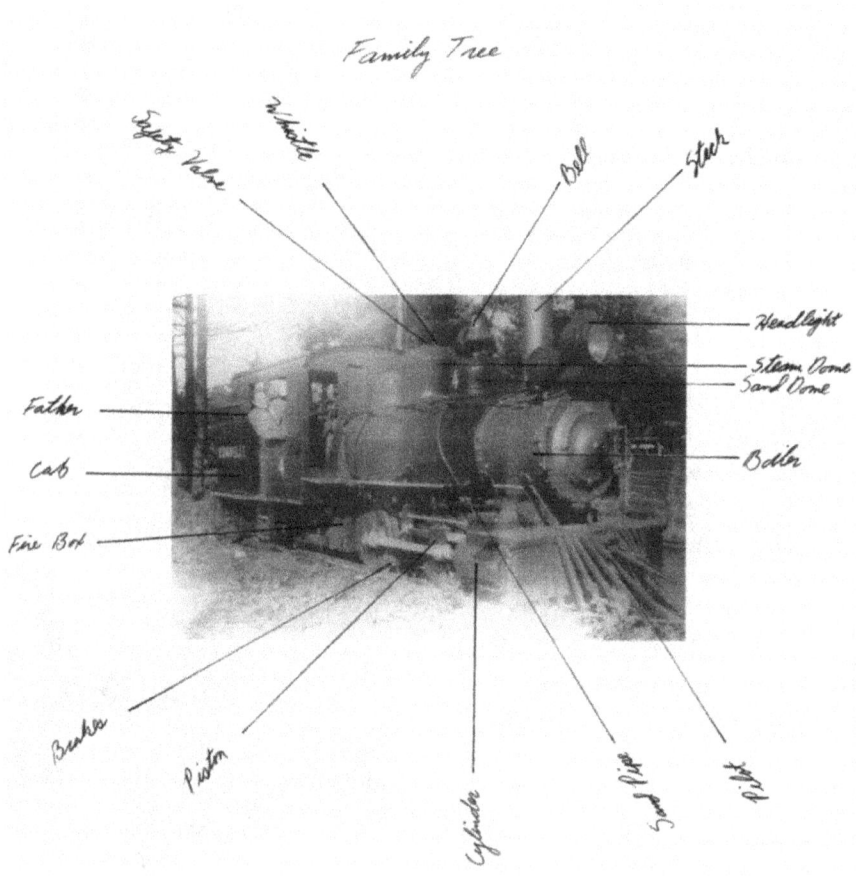

## Crossing the Divide

He traveled by train
capturing each scene
in half frame—
noting exposure,
speed, and location
en route to his final destination.

Each second here adds up to
only the present moment
as the landscape stands
completely still through the viewfinder,
with "1/100 sec" written on back
as he records the details of his journey—
the idle stretch of grasses,
and the regular progression
of post and rails.

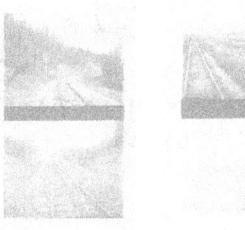

*one onehundredth one onehundredth*
"first hills of the Bitterroot range"
*one onehundredth one onehundredth*
"those rocks were amazing tints of pink and green"
*one onehundredth one onehundredth one onehundredth*
"Montana hills beginning to rise"
*one onehundredth one onehundredth one onehundredth*
"climbed several hours from the floor of the valley below"
*one onehundredth one onehundredth one*

In sequence, the tracks ascend
into a rise of mountains
border by stationary border
until he reaches the peak,
too high and light to photograph
without risk of overexposure,
it remains invisible to me.

In the rest of his prints, I
follow his eventual descent,
each shot now quickly
picking up the tracks
at a pace almost too rapid
to capture until we
finally arrive at
the sudden flatlands
where the exhaled images fade,
save one crossed post rising
out of the final frame.

**Proof**

These sailors,
among his portraits
of my grandparents,
look at him as if
he has lost his head—
distracting them
as they hurry aboard
the last train departing
from the railyard.

The body of his photography
remains unsorted, but
at last I've come to
view it through the
arrangement of his mind—
his parents,
my mother,
their children,
those Navy recruits,
among other characters
collected at the depot—
he greeted us all with
the same beneficence
he practiced at home,
generous almost to a fault,
at times neglecting his
wife and children's desire to
be distinguished as special,
leaving them wondering
who was foremost
in his thoughts.

Coming across these
seamen exposed in his
loose assembly of prints,
I am nearly as startled
as the bystanders witnessing
this spontaneous good nature
among strangers, and
I peer with them
toward the lens to
find a young man capturing
all the world with
a fleeting shutter
as he brings into focus
whomever may appear
before him, quickly advancing
the negative within
to develop
a positive
proof.

**"The Belle of Edenwald"**

Whenever I said that she
had won a beauty contest,
my mother was quick to correct
that it was based on talent, too,
*Sure, I was pretty,* she'd say,
as if any of her beauty had lapsed,
*But you had to have it all—*
eloquence, poise, *moxie,*
the ability to recite verse *in Latin.*

My grandmother had been a wallflower,
never donning the Chanel or silks
that my mother bought her as gifts,
keeping them *for good*
while her daughter shone,
sometimes in spite of herself,
unable to hold her tongue with her father,
or keep from laughing with her brother
at their somber family table.

She kept a list of the qualities
her future husband would possess,
and with her friend Beverly Smith
attended Wednesday dances to
scout them out—men not planning
a profession were immediately
dismissed in a quick exchange
between the two young women—
with a toss of curls over
her blond shoulder my
mother would simultaneously
snub the *fella* and signal to Bev
who would already be
pulling on her gloves,
elbows linked as they left together.

Weekends they spent studying,
memorizing their catechism,
preparing for the St. Barnabas parade,
or knitting uneven scarves for
someone who had *made the list,*
each joking he would never leave her
before his present was complete
for want of the warmth.
My mother couldn't sew
or cook either when
she was first wed,
for donations to bake sales
she purchased cheesecakes
from *Lindy's* on the corner,
and my father didn't care!

He saw her as a prize—
one who he'd won over,
gaining in her not solely
the adornment of the Belle
upon his arm, though,
Lord knows, he
loved that, too,
but the mettle that rang out
from inside of her,
constant and resonant,
so much so he was
barely able to hear,
during their departure
from *Our Lady of Assumption*
that twentieth day of June,
the carillon resounding
for the chime and cadence
of her laughter,
the rice falling
in time.

## Heart Failure

We have a history
in my family of
holding back our hearts—
unable to release the blood
in even measure to the vessels,
so it pools scarlet in our chambers
as grandfathers and sons face
each other through transparent walls
conserving their emotion and oxygen
until husbands leave their wives
as widows in these hospital halls
while daughters pace, expectant at home
and soon our brothers and nephews
splay exam tables, heads and legs
held steady by their mother's hands
in an attempt to ease the cessations
throughout these donations and transfusions—
as we draw blood from one another,
compensating for the hollows
of our hearts, that in forming,
never fully close one
against the other.

## Hey, Dad

*Hey, Dad,
you missed a spot,*
I call out to my father
pushing the reel mower
in the backyard
of the first house
we have ever owned.
My mother must have taken
this black and white
candid of him grinning,
thin, but not yet ill,
facing his prime,
without a trace of
sweat at his temple
even though the haze
nearly blots out the sun
this stagnant summer day.

In a light plaid shirt
with his sleeves rolled
to his elbows, and
belted slack khakis
cuffed at the ankle
of his work boots,
the laces wrapped once around,
he bends his head slightly
in concentration on the task.

I watch him propel the mower,
inching toward me so deft
and quickly that it seems he
never leaves his starting place,
but I hear the grinding of
the wheels and whirring rotor,
watch the sharpest blade
slice straight through the
turf at my father's feet,

a pungent gust stirring up
my sensitivity so forcefully
it startles me as my
eyes begin to well, and
I feel the tears streaming
until it becomes more
and more of an effort just
to breathe while I wait,
helpless but hopeful
my father will look up,
unbutton and withdraw
from his breast pocket
the white pressed handkerchief
he always kept with him,
extend it to me.

**Top this!**

Top this!
My father shook hands
with Albert Einstein
on the quad of Manhattan College
where Brother Leo introduced them—
my father graduating with
a degree in engineering,
Einstein's theories employed
in splitting the atom
the year they met—
Albert's greeting suspending itself
in the air over my father's head
like an awesome equation waiting
to be deciphered, understood:
Could Einstein actually be speaking to him?
My father responds, uncertain at first,
"It's such an honor..."
"I greatly admire..."
before finding his footing,
steadying his knees,
squaring his shoulders,
clearing his throat,
tightening his grip—
a firm handshake,
he remembers, is
the first gesture
of sincere character.

Afterward, my father must
have spirited his camera
into one of Einstein's lectures
since I have a hasty photograph
of the professor at the head of the class—
here is the explosion of wiry hair,
his weary zealous brow,

the grandfather collar that
has come undone from the stud
at the neck of his white shirt
wrinkled with distress, and
his crimped left elbow
that hangs like an injured wing
while his right arm, extended,
takes flight across the board
with seemingly ceaseless energy.
Using a magnifier
I try to decipher
the notes of this genius
amid the bits of dust
inherent in the blurry picture,
but his chalk inscriptions become
merely a profusion of tiny dots,
so profound in halftone pattern
that I cannot distinguish
one saturated particle from another—
the image before my eyes
wholly magnified yet
entirely incomprehensible.

So it's all relative—
I cannot confirm their meeting
since Brother Leo is long gone,
and my father's old roommate,
Uncle Harry, is only vaguely
able to recall the encounter;
he cannot say for certain it
is Einstein in the picture, although
he does not deny it either,
adding my father did carry
that Kodak all over, an
essential element
of life.

**Obituary**

In our urgency
to render her character,
my eldest brother and I
scrambled for organizations,
dates, and adjectives
to summarize my mother's
full and novel life within the
margin and deadline of obituary.

We wrote and reworked history
and chronology to flow into
the boundary of the column,
and get familial facts straight,
phoning relatives to locate
parish of baptism,
spell out her birthplace,
and fill in middle initials
of grandparents long gone.

My brother dictated it all back
as I typed, my fingers scarcely able
to keep up with the accolades.
We proofread two copies as
soon as I'd finished, our
heads bent and implements
poised in silence like
monks transcribing scripture,
fearfully exacting, lest
a passage be missed.

Just after the wake,
I came upon the one
she'd written for my father,
omitting education, achievements, survivors,
*A humble and dedicated man*
*to his God and work.*

All my years of writing,
and here she'd done it best,
including only those words
essential for others to
know him as she did.
I read it over again, and
found for all of its simple
eloquence, it lacked its other half—
*married to a woman,* I wrote,
*who wore his pride for him*
*in each of their children*
*she alone raised.*

## Plow

Out tonight amid the snow
and storm warnings
I watch the plow
come steaming by
and think immediately
of my father,
in the company of his machinery
lined up in preparation
at the department of transportation
in the cavernous garages
across the waving fields
on the summit of the hill
behind our house.
Ahead of me, the contact of
the steel against asphalt
raises sparks fierce
enough to strike fire
before casting aside the snow
like laden ashes.

He'd take pictures of the
equipment when it was new
or idle near a mass of earth
it had just surmounted,
and post them in his office
by his portraits of
my sister as an infant,
or elder brother posed
on the pitcher's mound.
The polished knobs
and toothy gears
of the plows,
the graders,
the sanders
appear willing
to take on any weather,
in parallel lines with my

siblings' eager smiles.

But the film belies
the sudden squall
of that harsh spring,
the dizzying winds
and darkened horizon
that descended on us,
found us without cover, or navigator,
immobilized and exposed
beneath a blanket of
ceaseless elements, unable
to dig ourselves out.

**Faithful**

A devout Catholic,
my mother ceased attending
mass after my father's funeral service.
Enduring hers, I understand
how those hymns that
suspend themselves on air,
reverberating like whispers
in her ear would make her
want to turn and look for him,
only to find polite acquaintances
with strained expressions of sympathy,
unease, and after they'd gone,
row upon empty row,
the clasp and nod of the priest
solemn but small solace as he
departed in a flurry of sash and robes
leaving her with my father's body,
a trace of incense
the last mingling
between them.

The following Sunday
I could hardly bear *Ave Maria*,
the high notes splitting like hysterics
in my head, impossible to listen
without thinking again
of the casket,
the eulogy,
the offerings,
of her spirit,
and where it might be,
where could I call on her now?

She must have wanted to ask him
endlessly about the children,
seek his opinion on
mundane and major decisions,
which shoes and what schools
in his absence would suit us best.
I want to ask her
if I do her justice as a writer,
if I will ever become a mother,
if she is at last free.

I want to tell her that
in a struggle to assemble
each week with the faithful,
I see it now—
her long lapse
not as irreverence
as I presumed
throughout adolescence,
but as a means of self-preservation—
faced with reliving his loss
or living without him,
she turned us out and
delivered us over
the threshold of St. Peter's
where she dared not dwell.

## Wind Chill

That winter,
the wind chill would not die;
I spent days inside, drifting
through the rooms of her things
unable to sort, compile,
or create an adequate shelter.
The wind would catch at
strands of my hair,
and I'd turn as if
toward an intruder,
hear it wailing from
between the shingles,
whipping around the windows,
flailing at the shutters
as if there were no walls.
Roused as if by siren,
I'd dress each morning
in woolen layers,
wrapping myself in,
bulking myself up,
diminishing myself
with each layer of insulation.
Even when the sun shone,
and I thought I might that day
evade it, the wind did not cease,
the panes of the porch door
caught in a glare
as the jamb and latch shook
in the hope or wake of
a saint or martyr.
I turned the almanac page,
found March steadily approaching,
and wondered how,
in the resounding roar of the lion,
I would be able to hear,
in the oncoming season,
the faithful bleating
of the lamb.

## Encircled by the Engraved Band

I never realized until this year
how difficult this ring
must have been for her to wear.
The platinum setting, raised emerald cut,
secured on either side by two baguettes,
encircled by the engraved band,
does not recede easily when
washing dishes, dressing children,
sleeping hand to cheek.

Even if she grew accustomed
to carrying its weight, the sparkle
from any bulb, mirror, or star
refracted, must have startled her,
the only brilliance of him remaining
those sleepless nights in the
house he'd built for them, the
children all tucked away.

When she willed it to me,
I thought it would be easy,
an honor to wear, providing
my hands the strength and agility
they'd lost engaging
in the everyday tedium that
seemed now magnified, the hardest matter.

Instead I catch it daily, closing
curtains, folding clothes, pulling on gloves
and it catches me unaware,
that facet of my life that cannot be refined—
it is lost forever, no mother,
no father, no longer
anybody's child.

I watch it glimmering,
wait for this symbol
to reveal, crystalline,
how, faced with such a loss,
she managed to reflect, endure.

I've tried to secure it,
but still the band slips
from side to side, moves
forward and back,
and I remember a gesture
so common, I'd forgotten,
she possessed of twisting
the band from beneath
to set the ring in
the middle of her finger
and thoughtfully consider
the four points extending
from the lucid center as
if to show the way.

**Landscaping**

The forsythia was her favorite—
the one he had planted
closest to the door,
the one she first saw
coming in or looking out
the paned glass, the one
she allowed an ecstatic
and grievous expression in
its upturned and dipping boughs,
left to its own design for
years after he, my
father, had died.

Forsythia was first to bloom
in spring, the first to suggest
a new season may indeed arrive,
and to prune it—slice through
the budding branches of
tiny yellow fists unfurling—
would have been to alter
the earth, the roots, the life
my father had planted there
as she had looked on,
expecting.

It wasn't the only wild one
in our yard—all those
she tended were given
room to grow, unbound,
their limbs, flora, wings unclipped,
the ground beneath me overrun
by stems and tenderfeet.

Below the untapered willow
he'd begun as a sapling,
I joined its weeping,
leaning back against its rough trunk,

feeling the shallow roots surface
at my feet, while the pointed leaves
occasionally stroked my shoulders,
at once startling and a comfort.

That stand of thin-skinned
birch provided little shade,
the sun striking the dappled bark—
bone white on gray ash
coming undone, scattering
in unforecasted gusts,
tempting me, year
after year, to peel
the layers back, expose
what was beneath,
providing some measure
of power over what
was allowed to live,
and what to perish.

Rows of tidy juniper
years on, eventually
grew into a refuge
of menacing and beckoning
arms around the porch,
the abrasive embrace
unforgiving, tight, piercing,
nearly leaving me scarred
whenever I sought
it out, so close and vibrant
I would contemplate

every sphere of berry—
hard, pungent, clustered, stubborn,
forbidden, and as she'd
often warned me, poisonous,
fatal, ever blue.

## Author's Note

> *"Such is the photograph: it cannot say what it lets us see."*
> —Roland Barthes, *Camera Lucida*

I have dedicated this volume to the honored memory of my father. Since he died when I was an infant, I have always derived material about his life from my family's collective memory, oral narrative, and snapshot photography. With these elements, I have been trying to piece his character together since I was a child when my mother and siblings repeated stories about him until I was old enough to tell them myself. Eventually, I began to wonder what my father's version of things might have been. I listened to the oral history over again in my mind, but I realized it was visual images I needed to flesh out my father's character.

I found myself delving into the cellar boxes that held his snapshot photography, peeling apart glossies and negatives, bending back curled corners of proofs, and recognizing selected family members and events. After hours of sorting, though, I realized most of the pictures, most of the well framed, carefully cropped pictures, were of railway trains. Model railroading was a lifelong hobby of my father's, but the hundreds of photographs I uncovered seem to reach beyond a pastime.

He carefully documented speeding segments of full-scale trains, trestle bridges, aftermath of wrecks, and empty stations, but the majority of his shots were composed of individual train cars that had been separated from their engines. There are cars of varied capacity and age: box cars at the beginning of the tracks, refrigerator cars in for repair, hopper cars hauling debris, stock cars derailed by storm, passenger cars set up on blocks, gondolas of bundled ties, work cars abandoned on dismantled bridges, and flat cars left on the tracks overgrown with weeds. Viewing these images intermingled with family pictures, I likened the stray cars to us, my father's children, who scattered in various directions after leaving our childhood home. I viewed our father, of course, as the engineer we had lost.

My father's work initially served as a departure point for me to enliven neglected images, but it came to mean even more as time went on. Closely examining each print, I saw my father's handwriting in smudged black pencil on the back of certain shots, referring to the setting and atmosphere, the speed of the f-stop, or the age of his firstborn child. My father's notes altered the strong and fair-minded man his legend had become, exposing a man subject to vulnerability and doubt. I even wondered if, in the throes of his urgent trips, he might have seen the end of his life quickly approaching at age forty-five.

I realized age was an ever-present factor for me, since I instinctively calculated my birthdate in relationship to the date on each print I found. As the youngest child, I was missing from most of my father's work, yet I continued to calculate, hoping to come across at least one previously undiscovered image of us occupying the same frame. Ultimately, I realized one image would never have sufficed. In the course of poring over the abundant number and spirit of his snapshots of everyday life, I realized it was the entire body of his photography which created his presence in my life. It allowed me not merely to illustrate the wide array of emotions, from longing to fulfillment, that his work evoked, but to sense and possess that once elusive connection to him, providing me with a tangible bond that will forever join us as father and daughter.

Megeen R. Mulholland received her Ph.D. from the University at Albany, and is a graduate of the Master of Arts program in English and Creative Writing at Binghamton University. She is a professor at Hudson Valley Community College where she teaches literature and writing. Her work has been published in *Journal of Poetry Therapy; Plath Profiles: An Interdisciplinary Journal for Plath Studies; Phoebe: A Journal of Feminist Scholarship, Theory, and Aesthetics; Roots and Flowers: Poets Write about Their Families;* and *Literary Mama: Reading for the Maternally Inclined*. Her first volume of poetry, titled *Orbit*, has been called an "epiphany of parenthood" and is available at Finishing Line Press and all booksellers.

www.ingramcontent.com/pod-product-compliance
Lightning Source LLC
LaVergne TN
LVHW041600070426
835507LV00011B/1208